# ENVIRONMENTAL DISASTERS

## MICHAEL WOODS AND MARY B. WOODS

LERNER PUBLICATIONS COMPANY
MINNEAPOLIS

To Douglas C. Neckers, Ph.D.

**Editor's note: Determining the exact death toll following disasters is often difficult—if not impossible—especially in the case of disasters that took place long ago. The authors and the editors in this series have used their best judgment in determining which figures to include.**

Lerner Publications Company
A division of Lerner Publishing Group, Inc.
241 First Avenue North
Minneapolis, MN 55401 U.S.A.

Website address: www.lernerbooks.com

Library of Congress Cataloging-in-Publication Data

Woods, Michael, 1946–
    Environmental disasters / by Michael Woods and Mary B. Woods
        p.    cm. —  (Disasters up close)
    Includes bibliographical references and index.
    ISBN-13: 978-0-8225-6774-5 (lib. bdg. : alk. paper)
    1. Environmental disasters—Juvenile literature.  2. Hazardous substances—Accidents—Juvenile literature.  3. Disasters—Environmental aspects—Juvenile literature.  4. Nuclear power plants—Accidents—Environmental aspects—Juvenile literature.  5. Tankers—Accidents—Environmental aspects—Juvenile literature.
    I. Woods, Mary B. (Mary Boyle), 1946–  II. Title.
    GE146.W66 2008
    363.7'02—dc22                                                    2006036730

Manufactured in the United States of America
1 2 3 4 5 6 – DP – 13 12 11 10 09 08

# Contents

# Introduction

MUYNAK WAS A CITY ON THE ARAL SEA. THIS CITY WAS IN UZBEKISTAN, A COUNTRY IN CENTRAL ASIA. IN 1960 FISHING BOATS CROWDED MUYNAK'S HARBOR. FISHERS SAILED ON THE ARAL'S SPARKLING WATERS EVERY DAY. BUT BY 2000, MUYNAK HAD NO FISH AND NO WATER. ITS BOATS WERE LEFT SITTING ON DRY LAND. ONE OF THE WORLD'S WORST ENVIRONMENTAL DISASTERS HAD TURNED THE LAND AROUND MUYNAK INTO A DESERT.

This fishing boat has been abandoned on the dry land that was once the bottom of the Aral Sea in Uzbekistan.

"Today the waters have receded [moved back] so much that there is not a drop as far as the eye can see," said Paul Welsh, a reporter for the British Broadcasting Corporation. "What was the fourth biggest inland sea is now mostly desert."

The disaster began in the 1960s. Goverment officials decided to grow cotton and other crops on some desert lands. They needed water to help the crops grow. Workers built canals to bring water to the crops. The water came from two rivers that flowed into the Aral Sea.

## THE SEA DISAPPEARED

Less and less water reached the Aral Sea. It began to dry up. More than half of the sea disappeared. People could walk on land that once was covered by water 60 feet (19 meters) deep.

The disaster affected more than 5 million people in the region. Fishers lost their jobs because fish disappeared from the sea. "The drying up of the Aral Sea has brought . . . people to their knees," said Khubbiniyaz Ashirbekov, head of the International Fund for the Saving of the Aral.

"The water has gone, and without it, we cannot even make bread. Illness and poverty have arrived."

Salt from the dried-up sea was left behind on the soil. Pollution from the water also remained in the dry seabed. Crops couldn't grow well in the poor conditions. "The land is barren, and salt covers the surface like snow," said Gaibull Mirzambekov, an official in the city of Nukus.

## A STORM OF DUST

Wind swept up the dry, polluted soil. Huge dust storms blew away more than 100 million tons (90 million metric tons) of dust from the seabed each year. People inhaled that salty, polluted dust. It also got into their food and drinking water. Thousands of people got sick.

"The human misery is huge," said Welsh. "Cancers, lung disease, and infant mortality [the death of babies] are 30 times higher than they used to be because the drinking water is heavily polluted."

In 2006 the government of Kazakhstan, another country on the Aral, built a dam and canals to make more water flow into the sea. Nobody knew if it would stop the disaster. The dam and canals did bring some water back to the Aral—but the land around Muynak remains a disaster zone. The sea is still much drier than it once was. And millions in the region still have trouble growing crops and finding clean water to drink.

The shrinking of the Aral has affected many people. It is a large-scale disaster.

These boats sit on what used to be the shore of the Aral Sea. The Aral dried up when it was drained to water crops.

5

# What Are Environmental Disasters?

ENVIRONMENTAL DISASTERS ARE DISASTERS THAT AFFECT THE NATURAL WORLD. THEY CAN MAKE THE WATER UNSAFE TO DRINK. THEY CAN DAMAGE THE LAND SO THAT PEOPLE MUST MOVE AWAY. SOME ENVIRONMENTAL DISASTERS CAUSE DAMAGE THAT LASTS FOR YEARS. OTHERS CAUSE ONLY SHORT-TERM DAMAGE.

Environmental disasters can be very destructive. They may kill or injure hundreds of people. They can damage things that people own. Environmental disasters may also harm wild animals, plants, and other things in the world around us.

## KILLER SPILLS AND LEAKS

There are several kinds of environmental disasters. Some of the worst involve spills or leaks of hazardous (dangerous) materials. These disasters usually happen suddenly.

In 2002 a ship carrying oil sank off the coast of Spain. About 2 million gallons (7.6 million liters) of oil spilled into the water. The sticky black oil washed onto beaches. It killed birds and other animals.

Poison gas leaked out of a factory in India in 1984. People living nearby breathed in the poison. Thousands of them became ill or died.

## DISH DUCK WASHER

How do you wash oil off birds and other animals? Most animal rescue workers use ordinary dish soap. They often like to use Dawn. This cleaner is strong but gentle on the animals' skin.

A rescue worker tries to clean oil off a bird.

Stones on this beach in Spain are covered with oil after the oil tanker the *Prestige* sank off the coast in 2002.

❝ *This is a disaster for the whole village. It will ruin many families.* ❞

—Jose Carrapero, a retired fisherman from Spain, on the 2002 Prestige oil spill

In 1986 radioactive material leaked from a nuclear power plant in Ukraine. About 335,000 people living nearby had to move. The radiation killed some people and made others very sick.

## SLOW DISASTERS

Other environmental disasters happen slowly. Farmland, for instance, may slowly change into desert. Lakes that provide fish may dry up. Factories may release pollution for years. The pollution may seem harmless. After years of building up, however, the pollution may reach harmful levels.

Slow environmental changes can be disastrous. They can make people starve to death. People also can be forced to leave home and move to a better place.

## MORE DISASTERS AHEAD?

Scientists believe that a slow environmental disaster is happening right now. Scientists worry about pollution from carbon dioxide. Carbon dioxide is a gas. It goes into the air when we burn fossil fuels. Fossil fuels power cars and trucks. They also bring heat and electricity to homes, schools, and businesses.

Carbon dioxide builds up over time. When it builds up, it traps heat near Earth's surface. The sun's rays shine on Earth. Some of the rays soak into the ground. Others bounce off the ground and go back into space. But carbon dioxide stops the rays from leaving Earth's atmosphere. It seals in the rays' heat so it cannot escape.

Carbon dioxide is changing Earth's climate (usual kind or pattern of weather). It is making Earth's climate grow warmer. The idea that Earth is getting warmer is known as global warming. Global warming can bring longer summers and milder winters to some parts of Earth.

A warmer climate might be good for some parts of the world. But in many ways, it could be very bad. Ice at the North Pole and the South Pole could melt. Water from the melted ice could raise ocean levels. Cities along the coasts could flood. The warmth also might bring severe weather. Warm air is a main ingredient in hailstorms, hurricanes, and tornadoes. That means global warming may cause more severe storms in the future.

Pollution from a power
plant in Germany

# 1914
# PASSENGER PIGEONS FLY INTO EXTINCTION

A group of men shoot at a large flock of passenger pigeons in Louisiana in this wood engraving from 1875.

John James Audubon saw a flock of wild pigeons flying through the air in 1813. He was a famous bird expert who then lived in Kentucky. The flock was enormous. It looked like a river flowing through the air. **"The air was literally filled with pigeons,"** Audubon said. **"The light of noon-day was [blocked out] as by an eclipse."**

The birds were passenger pigeons. They were beautiful animals. Passenger pigeons looked like mourning doves. But the birds were almost as big as chickens. They had blue heads, gray backs, red breasts, and scarlet eyes. Passenger pigeons ate acorns, beechnuts, chestnuts, fruits, grains, and insects. And they flew fast—60 miles (100 kilometers) per hour.

In 1813 passenger pigeons were the most common bird on Earth. About four out of every ten birds in North America were passenger pigeons. There were at least 5 billion passenger pigeons. Many people had Audubon's experience. They saw flocks 1 mile (1.6 km) wide and 300 miles (500 km) long.

It may seem impossible, but by 1913—just one hundred years later—there was only one passenger pigeon left on Earth. It was in a zoo and died in 1914.

How did the impossible happen? What kind of disaster could make an entire species of animal become extinct (die out forever)? The birds died partly because people cut forests to make room for farms. Passenger pigeons no longer had enough trees in which to build nests. Trees that grew acorns and other food for the birds also disappeared. But most of all, passenger pigeons became extinct because people hunted too many of the birds. Hunting them was easy. Whole flocks of passenger pigeons landed in one place. *"There would be so many pigeons [they'd] break the limbs off the trees,"* said Mary Ellen Walker, who grew up in a wooded area of southeast Texas. *"My two brothers would . . . bring pigeons [back home to eat] by the sack full. Just knock 'em out of the trees and bushes."*

In those days, there were no laws limiting the number of birds that could be killed. So people killed them by the thousands. In one part of Michigan, hunters killed fifty thousand passenger pigeons every day for five months.

People shot the birds with guns. One shot sometimes killed one dozen pigeons. People knocked them out of trees with sticks. They caught the pigeons in huge nets. People even exploded dynamite to kill flocks flying overhead.

Professional hunters killed passenger pigeons to sell. Trainloads of pigeons were shipped to big cities and sold in markets. Farmers fed the birds to their pigs. Some were used as fertilizer for fields. The dead bodies of those birds provided nutrients for crops. The death of such a huge number of animals was a terrible disaster.

## "The birds poured in in countless multitudes."

—John James Audubon describing the passenger pigeon, before the bird became extinct in 1914

Passenger pigeons were extremely common in the early 1800s.

# What Causes Environmental Disasters?

**MANY ENVIRONMENTAL DISASTERS HAPPEN BECAUSE OF HUMAN ERRORS. PEOPLE WHO WORK WITH HAZARDOUS MATERIALS GET TRAINING. THEY LEARN HOW TO KEEP DANGEROUS MATERIALS SAFELY INSIDE FACTORIES. BUT SOMETIMES WORKERS MAKE MISTAKES. DANGEROUS MATERIALS GET LOOSE IN THE ENVIRONMENT. THEN THESE MATERIALS CAUSE DISASTERS.**

In 2005 workers at a chemical factory in the city of Jilin in China made one mistake. They were supposed to shut off a valve (faucet). But they left it running. As a result, part of the chemical factory exploded.

## MAMMOTH MISTAKES

Five people were killed and sixty others were badly hurt in the Jilin factory explosion. Poisonous yellow smoke poured out from the factory. More than ten thousand people living nearby had to flee their homes.

About 100 tons (90 metric tons) of poison also leaked into the Songhua River. The poison flowed down the river toward the city of Harbin. More than 8 million people in Harbin got their drinking water from the Songhua River.

Water in the city had to be shut off for four days. People had to drink bottled water. They could not take showers or baths. People were very frightened. Nobody knows how many became ill because of the poison.

## MISTAKES HAPPEN

Mistakes happen for a number of reasons. Workers may not have learned the rules for handling dangerous materials. Or they might not follow the rules. Perhaps they have to make quick decisions in their jobs. The best choice isn't always clear. Although workers try hard, they sometimes make the wrong decision. Their actions may cause a disaster like the explosion in Jilin.

Smoke billows out of a chemical plant in Jilin, China, on November 13, 2005. More than ten thousand people had to leave their homes because of the poisonous smoke that came from the factory after part of it exploded.

# EQUIPMENT DISASTERS

Factories and other places with dangerous materials have safety equipment. That equipment keeps the dangerous materials from getting loose. Environmental disasters can happen when equipment breaks or does not work properly.

A nuclear disaster was narrowly avoided at Three Mile Island nuclear power plant, shown here in 1979.

A disaster almost happened when equipment broke at the Three Mile Island nuclear power plant in 1979. This Pennsylvania plant uses special pumps to cool its nuclear reactor (a machine in which nuclear energy is produced). One day the pumps stopped working. The nuclear reactor overheated. It got so hot that part of the reactor melted. Dangerous radiation almost escaped and contaminated the environment.

# MOTHER NATURE MISTAKES

Human errors that involve nature have caused some of the worst environmental disasters. In the late 1920s, people plowed up land in the Great Plains (a flat stretch of prairie in the central United States). They used the land to make huge farms. They also let millions of cattle graze on grasslands in the area.

It was a very unwise use of the land. Plowing and grazing destroyed grass that had covered the ground. Roots of the grass had helped keep the soil in place during dry weather.

When dry weather arrived in the 1930s, the area became extremely dusty. Wind swept away soil from parts of Texas, Oklahoma, Kansas, and other states. People began calling these states the dust bowl. Millions had to move away because they could not grow food on the desertlike land.

A dust storm blows into Stratford, Texas, on April 18, 1935. From 1931 to 1938, the weather was very dry in the Great Plains. Dust storms occurred often on the prairie.

# MULTIPLE CHOICE DISASTERS

Many environmental disasters have multiple causes. At Three Mile Island, for instance, water pumps broke and safety equipment was poorly designed. Workers could not tell right away that the nuclear reactor was getting too hot.

Almost 20 million gallons (80 million liters) of oil polluted beaches in Spain in 2002 when a storm cracked the hull (frame) of the *Prestige* oil tanker. The oil spill happened because the *Prestige* was not built well enough to withstand heavy waves. But government officials in Spain, France, and Portugal also played a role.

When the *Prestige*'s crew first discovered that the ship was damaged, they tried to sail to ports on land to have the damage repaired. But government officials didn't want the damaged ship to sail into their ports. They feared that oil leaking from the tanker would harm their land. The *Prestige* had to stay at sea. It eventually split in half and sank. The ship spilled far more oil than it would have had the damage been repaired.

## LOVE CANAL

**Bad judgment caused the Love Canal disaster in Niagara Falls, New York. Love Canal was a trench in the ground nearly 2 miles (3 km) long. In the 1920s, it became a dumping ground for toxic waste. About 22,000 tons (20,000 metric tons) of waste was buried there. When the trench was full, it was covered with clay and soil.**

**In the 1950s, people needed land for houses. They knew that toxic waste was buried at Love Canal. But people still built homes and a school on the land.**

**Soon poison began oozing up through the ground. Puddles of poison collected in the school playground and in basements of homes. People started getting sick. In 1978 a federal emergency was declared at Love Canal. Eventually, two hundred and twenty one families had to move.**

A bulldozer pushes soil away from one of the tanks used to bury toxic waste at Love Canal in New York.

The oil tanker the *Prestige* sinks off the coast of Spain on November 19, 2002. The tanker was carrying 60,000 tons (54,431 metric tons) of oil when it sank.

## FRIENDS AND FOES

Oil and other hazardous materials can cause serious disasters in the environment. But these materials aren't all bad. In fact, they can be very helpful when people use them properly.

Oil, for instance, is used to make gasoline. People also use it for making plastics and cloth. Oil is even used to make life-saving medicines.

Radioactive fuel in nuclear power plants is used to make electricity. Without nuclear power, we would have to rely more on coal and other fuels. These fuels cause air pollution.

Materials such as oil and radioactive fuel become hazards only when people use them improperly. When shipped, handled, or stored unsafely, they can become ingredients for environmental disasters.

## HUMAN HAZARDS

Hazardous materials can harm people, animals, and the environment in several ways. The chemical that leaked from a factory in Bhopal, India, for instance, was a poison. It was used to make insecticide (bug killer). When people breathed in the poison, they got sick, and many died.

Nuclear fuel gives off dangerous invisible rays. These rays can damage the intestines, blood, and other parts of the body. Some of the damage appears immediately. People exposed to enough nuclear rays may get radiation sickness within hours after exposure. Radiation sickness can cause vomiting, diarrhea, bleeding inside the body, and deadly infections.

Other symptoms of nuclear exposure may appear long after the disaster took place. Victims of nuclear disasters may develop cancer years later. If these people have children, their children may be born with health problems.

## FUR AND FEATHERS

You'd never guess how an oil spill harms animals with fur or feathers. Oil can make these animals freeze to death. How?

Two men carry injured children to a
hospital in Bhopal, India, after a leak
at a chemical plant in December 1984.

"Mothers didn't know their children had died,
children didn't know their mothers had died,
and men didn't know
their whole families had died."

—Ahmed Khan, who lived in Bhopal, India,
during the poison gas leak of 1984

Fur and feathers act like winter coats for animals. They keep animals warm by trapping air near their bodies. But when oil gets on animals, it soaks into their fur or feathers. It turns their coats into a greasy mess. To trap air, fur and feathers must stay fluffy. Without their natural coats, animals get cold and die.

## OIL FOR DINNER?

Some animals may be hurt by eating oil. They may eat oil while trying to clean it off their feathers or fur. Eagles, wolves, and bears may swallow oil when eating oil-soaked animals.

Oil is toxic. Eating oil can kill animals immediately. It also can weaken animals so that they die long after an oil spill.

An oil spill can harm large animals by killing the small animals that they eat. Oil spills can kill clams, snails, and worms, for instance. These smaller creatures are food for fish, birds, and other animals.

### ONE–PERSON DISASTER

Could one person cause an environmental disaster? It may have happened in Times Beach, Missouri. Everyone in this town of 2,240 people had to move away in the 1980s. The soil was contaminated with a chemical called dioxin. How did it happen?

Times Beach's dirt roads got dusty in the summer. In the 1970s, the city hired a man to spray the roads with oil from a truck. He used oil contaminated with dioxin. The government cleaned up the dioxin. Then, in 1999, it turned Times Beach into Route 66 State Park.

U.S. Environmental Protection Agency workers take soil samples from lawns and streets in Times Beach, Missouri, in 1983.

An African penguin is covered with oil after a tanker sank off the coast of South Africa in 2000.

# 1952 LONDON'S KILLER SMOG

Pigeons flock around pedestrians in London's fog-shrouded Trafalgar Square on December 7, 1952.

In the 1950s, people in London, England, burned coal to heat their homes. The coal burned in stoves. The stoves had chimneys, as fireplaces do. Smoke from the burning coal went up the chimneys. It rose into the air and blew away.

But on December 5, 1952, the smoke didn't blow away. On that day, fog rolled into London. A layer of warm air formed high above the city. The warm air acted like the lid on a pot. It trapped the smoke. Instead of rising, the smoke collected in the air. The pleasant, clean fog became a thick, yellow-green cloud of poison.

*"It was the worst fog that I'd ever encountered,"* said Barbara Fewster, then a young ballet dancer in London. *"It had a yellow [color] and a strong, strong smell . . . because it was really pollution from coal fires that had built up. Even in daylight, it was a ghastly yellow color."*

People could not see their hands in front of their faces. *"It's like you were blind,"* remembered Stan Cribb, who was working in London when the fog hit. People with lanterns had to walk in front of buses and cars to guide them. Drivers abandoned their cars in the streets. Trains and buses stopped running.

The choking fog even got inside buildings. Schools, stores, and theaters closed because people could not see. Barry Linton, aged seven, went home from school to find the fog had invaded his house. *"Even in our . . . living room, it was misty and choky,"* Linton remembered. *"And every time I blew my nose, it looked like soot in my hanky."*

People realized they were breathing in unhealthful air. A walk though the fog turned Fewster's clothing black. *"I was wearing a . . . yellow scarf and that too was pitch black with soot and muck,"* she said. *"Our faces were black, our noses were black, and everything was filthy."* People wore cloth masks to protect their noses and mouths.

But nobody imagined just how harmful the fog truly was. *"There weren't bodies lying around in the street, and no one really noticed that more people were dying,"* said Dr. Robert Waller, who worked in a London hospital. But indeed, the fog was making people very sick. And those sickened by the fog could not get to hospitals. They died in their homes. The first sign of a disaster was when London began to run out of coffins to bury people.

On December 9, the weather finally changed, and the fog blew away. Only then did doctors realize that the fog had killed almost four thousand people. London's killer smog was one of the worst environmental disasters in the twentieth century.

*"*The smog hit us like a wall.*"*

—Barbara Fewster, on London's killer smog

A London police officer wears a special mask to protect him from smog.

# Disaster Country

ENVIRONMENTAL DISASTERS USUALLY HAPPEN IN CERTAIN PLACES. THOSE PLACES ARE NEAR LARGE AMOUNTS OF HAZARDOUS MATERIAL THAT CAN SPILL OR LEAK. THE HAZARDOUS MATERIAL MAY BE IN A CHEMICAL FACTORY OR A NUCLEAR POWER PLANT.

Hazardous material also may move from one place to another. Oil tankers, for instance, carry crude oil for long distances over the ocean. Trains move tanker cars filled with chemicals.

When an oil tanker or train is carrying hazardous materials, a spill or leak could happen anywhere along the vehicle's path. People and animals living nearby are in the danger zone for an environmental disaster.

## CLOSE-RANGE DISASTERS

Environmental disasters often happen in a small area near a factory or other source of hazardous materials. When poison gas leaked from a chemical plant in Bhopal, India, for example, only those living near the plant were hurt. As the gas drifted through the air, it became weaker. It was not strong enough to hurt people elsewhere in Bhopal.

## A BIRD NAMED MARTHA

By 1901 the only passenger pigeons in the world lived in zoos. One was named Martha (*below*). She lived in the Cincinnati Zoo in Ohio. Martha died on September 1, 1914. With her death, passenger pigeons became extinct. Martha's body was stuffed and sent to the Smithsonian Institution in Washington, D.C.

Only two hundred and twenty one families were affected by the Love Canal disaster near Niagara Falls, New York. People living in the Love Canal neighborhood had to move. But the disaster did not affect the entire city of Niagara Falls.

## FAR-RANGE DISASTERS

Environmental disasters don't always stick to small areas. Sometimes they affect people farther away. The size of the disaster zone depends on the amount of hazardous material that is released. It also depends on the kind of material.

## DID YOU KNOW?

Chemical leaks and spills have caused terrible disasters. However, that's not a reason to fear all chemicals. Chemicals are very important in everyday life. Medicines, food, clothing, soap, computers, and cell phones are all made from chemicals. In fact, everything in the world is a chemical. Even people are made from chemicals.

Wind blew radioactive dust from a 1986 nuclear disaster in Chernobyl, Ukraine, hundreds of miles across Europe. The dust remained dangerous for many months. Small amounts of Chernobyl radiation even reached the United States.

Oil washed up on 1,300 miles (2,100 km) of Alaska's beaches and shores when the *Exxon Valdez* oil tanker crashed near Alaska in 1989. Oil spills can be especially wide-ranging disasters. That's because oil floats on water. Oil also spreads out in a thin layer called a slick. Ocean currents spread oil slicks over large areas.

This image shows a simulation of where radioactive material from the Chernobyl plant had spread around the globe ten days after the disaster.

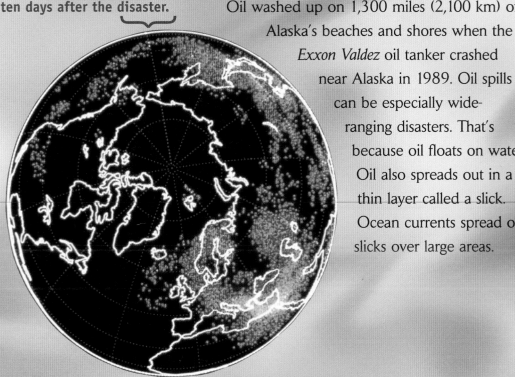

# DISASTER ZONES

Environmental disasters often happen near nuclear power plants or factories where large amounts of chemicals are present—but they can happen anywhere around the world. This map shows where some notable environmental disasters have taken place.

CHERNOBYL (Ukraine)
1986
(5 million+ people affected)

ARAL SEA (Uzbekistan)
1960s–present
(5 million+ people affected)

EUROPE

ASIA

JILIN (China)
2005
(10,000+ people affected)

LONDON (England)
1952 (about 4,000 deaths)

AFRICA

BHOPAL (India)
1984 (19,000+ deaths)

AUSTRALIA

PRINCE WILLIAM SOUND
(Alaska) 1989
(250,000+ wild animals
affected)

NORTH AMERICA

NIAGARA FALLS (New York)
1978 (221 families affected)

TIMES BEACH (Missouri)
1980s
(2,240+ people affected)

SOUTH AMERICA

The factory in Bhopal, India, where the poison gas leaked in 1984.

## 1984
# POISON GAS LEAK IN BHOPAL

Rashida Bee and her family went to bed early on December 3, 1984. They lived in Bhopal, India. Everyone slept soundly until just after midnight. Then a noise from her children's bedroom woke Bee. It was the sound of the children coughing—loud, frightening coughs.

*"They said they felt like they were being choked,"* Bee remembered. *"One of the children opened the door, and a cloud came inside. We all started coughing violently, as if our lungs were on fire."*

Thousands of other people in Bhopal were waking up sick because of that same cloud. It was a cloud of poison gas. The gas was released in an explosion at a factory. When the cloud of gas rolled in, people ran for their lives.

*"The panic was so great that as people ran, mothers were leaving their children behind to escape the gas,"* said Champa Devi Shukla, a resident of Bhopal. When people tripped and fell, nobody stopped to help them. They got trampled by the crowd.

*"It felt like somebody had filled our bodies up with red chilies,"* said Shukla. *"Our eyes [had] tears coming out, [our] noses were watering, [and] we had froth [foam] in our mouths."*

People could not see because the gas was as thick as fog. The gas also burned their eyes like fire. *"Our eyes were so swollen that we could not open them,"* said Bee. *"After running half a kilometer [0.3 miles], we had to rest. We were too breathless to run, and my father had started vomiting blood."*

When the panicked crowd passed, it left the streets littered with the bodies of people who were dead or dying. Dead dogs, cats, and other animals also lined the streets. The gas had poisoned the animals.

People ran toward hospitals. There were five hospitals in Bhopal, and all were quickly crowded. Chaos set in as patients streamed through the doors. Some were screaming and crying. Others were choking to death. Doctors were not sure how to treat the patients. Officials at the chemical company did not tell the doctors what was in the gas.

Nobody knows how many people died in the days immediately following the disaster. It was at least 4,000 people, and perhaps as many as 10,000. Somewhere between 200,000 and 500,000 people were injured. At least 15,000 of these people later died. Others became so ill than they could not work, go to school, or take care of themselves.

Thousands of animals died when the gas leaked from the factory in India.

> ## The room was filled with a white cloud. . . . Each breath [seemed] as if I was breathing in fire.

—Aziza Sultan, recalling the 1984 gas leak in Bhopal

The shantytowns around the factory were the hardest hit by the poison gas leak in 1984.

29

# Measuring Environmental Disasters

**MEASURING ENVIRONMENTAL DISASTERS IS IMPORTANT. MEASUREMENTS HELP OFFICIALS LEARN HOW SEVERE A DISASTER IS. WHEN OFFICIALS HAVE THIS INFORMATION, THEY MAY BE ABLE TO STOP A DISASTER BEFORE IT'S TOO LATE.**

Measuring environmental disasters also helps officials know what steps to take to correct a problem. Imagine what might have happened if someone had measured how many passenger pigeons were being hunted. Governments might have realized that the passenger pigeon was becoming extinct. They could have made laws to stop hunters from killing so many birds.

## DISASTER SCALES

Measuring environmental disasters is useful, but it is not always easy. It isn't like measuring a hurricane or tornado. For these types of disasters, there are scales to weigh the event—much like a bathroom scale weighs a person. Disaster scales tell officials all about a disaster. They also can help the officials plan for future disasters.

## DISASTER DISEASE

One disease is named for an environmental disaster. It is Minamata disease. Minamata disease sickened people in the town of Minamata, Japan *(above)*. The disaster began in 1932. A factory started polluting the water of Minamata Bay with mercury. This poisonous material got into fish in the bay. When people ate the fish, they were poisoned. Thousands of people in Minamata were still suffering from mercury poisoning in 2007.

Environmental workers clean up a chemical spill in Virginia.

But there are no scales to weigh environmental disasters. And environmental disasters also may have no sudden start or end. It may take years to realize that an environmental disaster has begun.

## COUNTING BODIES

In spite of these challenges, scientists do have ways of measuring environmental disasters. They can measure them by looking at how much damage they cause. Most important is the number of people who are harmed in the disaster. People may be killed or injured.

The Bhopal, India, chemical leak certainly was a worse disaster than London's killer smog. Why? It was worse because more people died and were injured in Bhopal than in London.

## COUNTING MONEY

Disasters cause damage to buildings and other property. It costs money to fix that damage. The amount of damage is another way to measure environmental disasters.

The Chernobyl nuclear accident killed or injured thousands of people. It also caused enormous damage to property. People could no longer live within 20 miles (30 km) of the plant.

People lost their homes because of Chernobyl. They could

## PUT A LID ON IT

Workers limited damage from the Chernobyl disaster. They built walls around the damaged plant. The walls prevented more radiation from getting out. In 2006 workers were building strong new walls. These walls should keep a lid on Chernobyl for at least one hundred years.

An aerial view of the Chernobyl Nuclear Power Plant in 2006.

This collective (shared) farm near Chernobyl was abandoned after the disaster in 1986.

"There was fear inside us all as we knew we were dying there. A metal taste in my mouth and it felt like someone was touching my body all over from inside, muscles, bones, everything."

—Anatoly Zakharov, a firefighter who helped battle the flames at the Chernobyl nuclear disaster in 1986

not farm the land or sell their crops. According to one estimate, Chernobyl caused hundreds of billions of dollars in damage.

## COUNTING NATURE

We also measure environmental disasters based on how much they hurt Earth and wildlife. In 2004 oil leaked from the *Selendang Ayu,* a ship sailing off the coast of Alaska. Up to 340,000 gallons (1.3 million liters) of oil may have leaked into the water. Rescue workers found about 1,600 birds that had been killed by the oil.

About 11 million gallons (42 million liters) of oil leaked in the 1989 *Exxon Valdez* disaster. That oil killed about 250,000 birds. Which disaster was worse?

## COUNTING TIME

Time is another measure of a disaster's severity. Nature can recover from some disasters. Spilled oil, for instance, slowly disappears. Animals that survived an oil spill reproduce and replace the animals that died.

The effects of other disasters last and last. Land near the Chernobyl Nuclear Power Plant may never be safe enough for people to return. And once the passenger pigeon became extinct, it was gone forever.

*(Top)* The freighter ship the *Selendang Ayu* broke apart off the coast of Alaska in 2004, spilling thousands of gallons of oil. *(Bottom)* Rescue workers collect dead birds from an oily beach in France after the tanker ship *Erika* wrecked off the coast in 1999.

Workers clean oil off a beach in France in 1999.

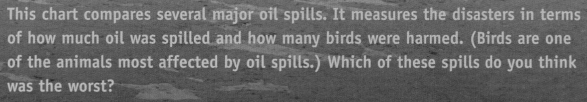

This chart compares several major oil spills. It measures the disasters in terms of how much oil was spilled and how many birds were harmed. (Birds are one of the animals most affected by oil spills.) Which of these spills do you think was the worst?

| NAME OF OIL TANKER | YEAR AND LOCATION OF SPILL | AMOUNT OF OIL SPILLED | NUMBER OF BIRDS HARMED |
|---|---|---|---|
| TORREY CANYON | 1967, NEAR GREAT BRITAIN | ABOUT 30 MILLION GALLONS (113 MILLION L) | 15,000+ |
| AMOCO CADIZ | 1978, NEAR FRANCE | ABOUT 69 MILLION GALLONS (261 MILLION L) | 300,000+ |
| EXXON VALDEZ | 1989, NEAR ALASKA | ABOUT 11 MILLION GALLONS (42 MILLION L) | 250,000+ |
| PRESTIGE | 2002, NEAR SPAIN | ABOUT 20 MILLION GALLONS (80 MILLION L) | 300,000+ |
| SELENDANG AYU | 2004, NEAR ALASKA | ABOUT 340,000 GALLONS (1.3 MILLION L) | 1,600+ |

The remains of the nuclear reactor that exploded at the Chernobyl Nuclear Power Plant in 1986

# 1986
# CHERNOBYL NUCLEAR DISASTER

**W**hen Nadezhda Vygovskaya woke up on April 26, 1986, it seemed like just another beautiful spring morning. Vygovskaya lived in Pripyat, Ukraine. Pripyat was about 80 miles (130 km) north of Kiev, Ukraine's capital city.

*"I sent my son to school, my husband went to the barber's,"* Vygovskaya remembered. *"I'm preparing lunch when my husband comes back. 'There's some sort of fire at the nuclear plant,' he says. 'They're saying we are not to turn off the radio.'"*

Vygovskaya never dreamed that she was witnessing one of the world's worst environmental disasters. But indeed, a tragedy was unfolding in Pripyat that day. It had started in the wee hours of the morning.

At 1:23 A.M., an explosion had happened at the nearby Chernobyl Nuclear Power Plant. Chernobyl produced electricity for Ukraine. The plant used nuclear fuel to make electricity. The fuel was radioactive.

The explosion caused the radioactive fuel to escape from the plant. The blast had torn huge holes in Chernobyl's walls and roof. Radioactive material seeped through the holes. The explosion also had started fires. More radioactive material escaped in the smoke. Wind carried the radioactive material away like a cloud of dust.

As Vygovskaya and other people nearby were going about their business, the dust was dropping down on them. *"We knew nothing all day,"* said Lyubov Kovalevskaya, who lived in Pripyat. *"Nobody said anything. Well, they said there was a fire. But about radiation, that radioactivity was escaping, there was not a word."*

Firefighters at the Chernobyl plant also were not aware of the danger. They fought the fires without putting on special suits. The suits could have protected firefighters from the radiation. At least forty seven of these workers died from radiation exposure.

Much of the radioactive dust fell on the ground near Chernobyl. Everyone

In 1989 a woman holds out a newly born pig that has deformities related to the Chernobyl explosion.

living within 20 miles (30 km) of Chernobyl—135,000 people—had to be evacuated (moved to a safer place). Later on, more than 200,000 other people also had to move away.

Wind blew the radioactive dust far away from Chernobyl. The dust remained dangerous for years. It contaminated farm animals. In some cases, it caused the animals to develop abnormally. *"At the . . . Petrorovsky collective farm, I was shown a [baby] pig whose head looked like that of a frog,"* one newspaper report wrote. The radiation made milk, meat, fruits, and vegetables unsafe to eat. Farmers could not sell these foods. They lost billions of dollars.

More than 5 million people were living on land contaminated by the accident. Contaminated land can increase people's risk for developing diseases. It can take years for these diseases to appear. Doctors are not sure how many people will someday get sick because of the contamination.

# People Helping People

WHEN A DISASTER STRIKES, THE VICTIMS NEED HELP. THEY USUALLY NEED THREE DIFFERENT KINDS OF ASSISTANCE: RESCUE, RELIEF, AND RECOVERY. RESCUE MEANS HELPING THE VICTIMS OUT OF A DISASTROUS SITUATION. RELIEF MEANS REDUCING THE AMOUNT OF SUFFERING AMONG THE VICTIMS. RECOVERY MEANS HELPING PEOPLE GET THEIR LIVES BACK TO NORMAL.

Victims need this help fast. A fast response to victims' needs can prevent a bad disaster from getting worse. Paramedics, for instance, can save the lives of people who are injured. Rescue workers can free people who are trapped at a disaster scene. Relief workers can provide clean water, food, and other help to reduce the suffering of victims.

When the emergency is over, disaster victims often need help to recover. Homes and other buildings must be repaired or rebuilt. Some people may have to find a new place to live or work.

A worker sprays water on canvas screens set up around the chemical plant in India in 1984.

## DIFFICULT DISASTERS

Rescue, relief, and recovery work can be especially difficult in environmental disasters. In addition to the human victims, thousands of wild animals may need assistance. And the damage in an environmental disaster may cover a huge area. When the tanker *Prestige* sank near Spain in 2002, for example, oil spilled into the water. The oil

Volunteers clean oil off a beach in Spain after the *Prestige* sank off the coast in 2002.

washed up onto more than one thousand beaches across Spain and France.

## DISASTER RESPONSE

In environmental disasters, assistance comes from many different sources. In an oil spill, government agencies often get involved. Special teams from the U.S. Coast Guard respond to oil spills along the shore. For oil spills in inland waters, the U.S. Environmental Protection Agency is in charge.

Local fire departments, police, and other emergency workers also respond to environmental disasters. Many areas have hazardous materials teams, or hazmat teams. These workers are specially trained to respond to chemical spills. The American Red Cross, churches, and many private groups help too.

## A MASSIVE SPILL

Enough oil spilled in the *Exxon Valdez* disaster *(below)* to fill about nine school gyms from floor to ceiling.

## LIMITING THE DAMAGE

The ways in which workers respond to a disaster depend on what kind of disaster has occurred. A response that works for a chemical spill is not appropriate for a radioactive leak.

No matter what type of disaster has taken place, workers first try to limit the damage. They might start by plugging up a leak. Or they might try to keep the dangerous material at the disaster scene. If the material spreads, it will cause a worse disaster. Oil, for instance, floats on the surface of water. If workers don't contain it, it will drift far away.

## BOOMS AND FLAMES

Workers responding to an oil spill often place booms in the water. Booms are floating barriers that can keep spilled oil from spreading. Some booms

U.S. Environmental Protection
Agency workers clean up a site
near Houston, Texas.

are inflatable rubber tubes that form a wall around the oil. The wall usually is about 3 feet (1 m) high. It is high enough to keep waves from spreading the oil.

Booms, or floating barriers, surround the oil spilled from the *Exxon Valdez* near Alaska in 1989.

Once the oil spill is surrounded, workers try to remove the oil. They may use special hoses to suck up the mess. Or they might trap the spilled oil inside a fireproof boom. Then they set the oil on fire. Workers set oil on fire after the *Exxon Valdez* disaster. The fire helped remove some of the oil. But stormy weather spread the rest of the oil far away.

## SUPER SOPPER-UPPERS

Workers may pour dispersants on an oil spill. Dispersants are chemicals that break oil into small droplets. The droplets quickly disappear. Dispersants help reduce the damage caused by oil spills.

Workers also might use absorbent materials to sop up spilled oil. Absorbent materials soak up liquids. They keep liquids from spreading. Good oil sopper-uppers include straw, sawdust, ground corncobs, and chicken feathers. When poured on an oil spill, these materials absorb oil in much the same way that a sponge absorbs a spilled drink.

## HELPING PEOPLE AND ANIMALS

As officials work to contain a disaster, they also assist those affected by the tragedy. Rescue workers often evacuate people living near a chemical spill or nuclear accident. In an evacuation, people move away from the disaster scene. They stay away until it is safe to return home.

In big cities, evacuation may be impossible. The roads would be jammed. More people might be hurt in accidents than in the disaster itself. Instead of evacuating, people in cities may stay where they are—at home or in school.

Many people need medical care after a disaster. People might need medicines to help prevent harm from chemicals or radiation. Or they

Fire bombs were dropped on the oil tanker the *Torrey Canyon* in 1967. Workers were trying to burn off the oil that was leaking from the sinking ship off the coast of Great Britain.

might need to wash dangerous materials off their skin. Particles of certain kinds of radiation can be washed off. Washing also can remove certain hazardous chemicals.

Assisting wild animals after a disaster can be tricky. The animals are frightened of people. They don't know that the people are trying to help.

Workers take injured animals to treatment centers. If the animals are contaminated, the workers wash them off. Then they put them into warm cages in a quiet area. The animals have had a lot of stress. They need rest and food. When the animals recover, they are released into an area away from the disaster.

## RECOVERY

It is easy to tell when you have recovered from a cold or another illness. But it can be hard to tell when the environment has recovered from a disaster.

In some cases, officials may not know what an area was like before a disaster struck. It can be hard to know if an area has recovered if no one knows what it was like before the damage occurred.

In other cases, recovery seems to have happened—but the area may suffer lasting effects. The area affected by the *Exxon Valdez* spill, for example, began to look better shortly after the accident took place. Within three years, almost no oil could be seen on beaches and shores. However, scientists could still detect signs of damage in the area almost twenty years after the accident. Would you say that recovery has occurred?

Rescuers tend to a cormarant after the *Exxon Valdez* accident.

**"*It's pathetic.* There's dead otters. There's dead scoters [seabirds]."**

*—Rick Steiner, who saw animals struggling to get out of thick oil during the Exxon Valdez oil spill in 1989*

Oil from the *Exxon Valdez* swirls on the surface of the water of Prince William Sound in Alaska on April 9, 1989.

# 1989
# THE *EXXON VALDEZ* OIL SPILL

The *Exxon Valdez* was an oil supertanker. These ships are giant floating tanks. They carry crude oil from one place to another. The *Exxon Valdez* was 987 feet (301 m) long, longer than three football fields. It held about 53 million gallons (200 million liters) of oil.

On March 24, 1989, the *Exxon Valdez* was sailing through Prince William Sound in Alaska. This area was famous for its natural beauty. Millions of fish, birds, seals, sea lions, and other wildlife lived there.

Just after midnight, the *Exxon Valdez* turned to avoid hitting icebergs. But the ship turned too far. It crashed into rocks. They ripped the *Exxon Valdez*'s steel bottom open like a can of soda pop. Oil poured out of the ship and into the water of Prince William Sound.

*"I saw her there on the rocks,"* remembered Chuck O'Donnell, who arrived on the scene shortly after the crash. *"Crude oil was just [pouring] out. I knew it was a disaster, seeing all that oil on the water."*

Dan Lawn of the Alaska Department of Environmental

Animals such as sea lions *(left)* and sea otters *(below)* struggled in the oily water after the spill.

"We've fetched up hard aground.

# We're leaking some oil, "

## and we're going to be here for a while.

—Joseph Hazelwood, captain of the **Exxon Valdez**, *to the* **Coast Guard** *on March 24, 1989*

Conservation sailed out to the *Exxon Valdez* to check on the damage. He found oil about 3 feet (1 m) deep floating on the water. **"It was kind of like having your nose in the gas tank of your car,"** Lawn said of the smell the oil spill produced.

Almost 11 million gallons (42 million liters) of oil spilled into the water. The oil spread over Prince William Sound. To make matters worse, a storm blew in with winds of more than 70 miles (110 km) per hour. Wind and waves washed oil onto almost 1,300 miles (2,100 km) of beaches along the Alaska coast. Oil was knee-deep on some beaches.

The heavy oil coated the feathers of birds so they could not fly. Some of them drowned. Seals and sea otters that caught food by diving into the water got stuck in the goop. Some of them also drowned.

Jay Holcomb and Kelly Weaverling rescued birds caught in the spill. **"It was so gross,"** remembered Holcomb. **"A bird would fly in, it would start to struggle, and then it would go under [the water]."**

Weaverling couldn't believe the scene. **"Dead otters. Dead deer. Dead birds,"** he said of what he saw. **"We cried a lot. All of us did, at least once, maybe twice a day."**

Crude oil is not just messy. It also can poison animals. At least 250,000 seabirds, 2,800 sea otters, 300 seals, 250 bald eagles, and 22 orcas (killer whales) died in the oil spill. The oil also destroyed billions of eggs that would have hatched into salmon and other fish.

# The Future

**IN THE 1970S, SCIENTISTS DISCOVERED THAT A TERRIBLE ENVIRONMENTAL DISASTER HAD BEGUN. CHEMICALS IN AEROSOL SPRAY CANS WERE CAUSING THE DISASTER. PEOPLE USED THESE CANS TO SPRAY UNDERARM DEODORANT, AIR FRESHENER, AND OTHER PRODUCTS.**

The chemicals drifted up into the air and began to destroy the ozone layer. The ozone layer forms an invisible protective shield high in Earth's atmosphere. It keeps harmful ultraviolet (UV) rays from reaching Earth's surface.

If the ozone layer were destroyed, more UV rays would get through to Earth. The rays would make people get skin cancer and other diseases. Plants and animals also would be harmed.

## DISASTERS THAT NEVER HAPPEN

The disaster was stopped just in time. Scientists discovered that the chemicals were harmful. They warned people about this danger. Countries around the world agreed to stop using the dangerous chemicals.

Modern-day aerosol spray cans use safe chemicals. These chemicals do not damage the ozone layer. The ozone is slowly recovering from damage done in the past.

In the future, scientists may know how to spot the early warning signs of other environmental disasters. Those disasters may be just starting. But with a lot of research and a little luck, these disasters will end before it's too late—just like the ozone crisis.

Aerosol cans such as this one contained chemicals that were harmful to the environment.

A woman gets her hair sprayed with a product from an aerosol can in 1957.

## MOTHER EARTH'S HEALTH

In 2005 more than sixty countries in the world started a new project. This project could prevent future environmental disasters. It is called the Global Earth Observation System of Systems (GEOSS).

Has the doctor ever listened to your heartbeat? GEOSS will help scientists listen to Earth's heartbeat. It will help them see if planet Earth is healthy or sick.

Earth observation systems are instruments and other tools. They give us information about the planet. These instruments measure air contamination, water pollution, and many other environmental threats. Some of these instruments are on airplanes or satellites that orbit Earth. Others are on the ground or in the oceans.

## EARLY WARNING SIGNALS

The instruments make millions of measurements of Earth every day. In the past, there was no way to share the measurements. Scientists in the United States didn't know what scientists in Europe had found.

GEOSS will change that. By 2010 it will let scientists in different countries see all the measurements. Scientists will be able to better study Earth's health.

Those studies will help scientists see how people are affecting Earth. They will be able to spot dangerous changes, such as weakening of the ozone shield. When scientists see warning signs of disastrous changes, countries can act to prevent disasters.

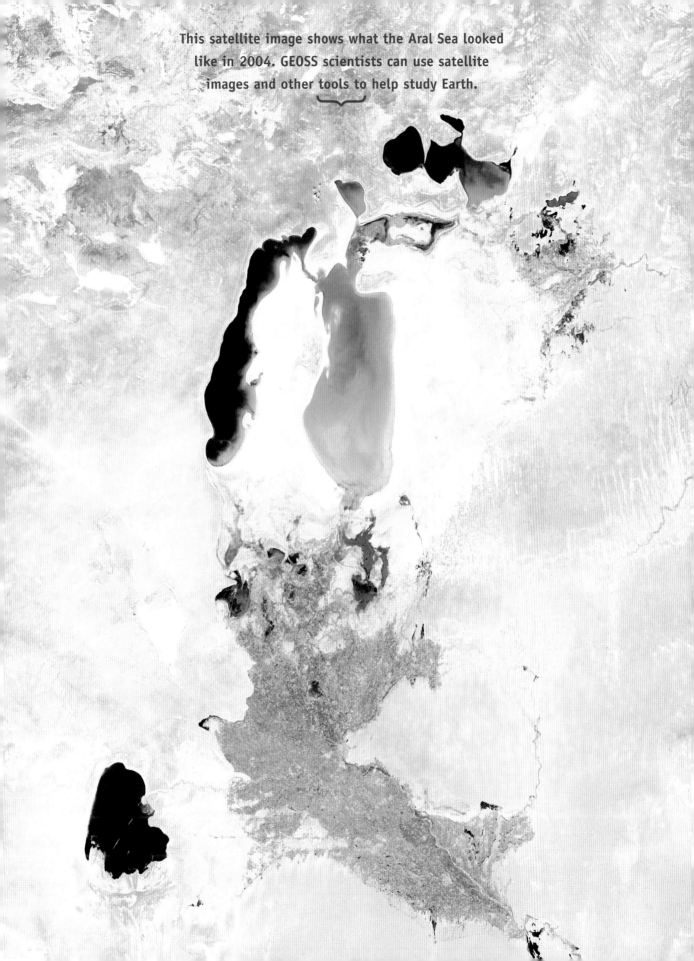

This satellite image shows what the Aral Sea looked like in 2004. GEOSS scientists can use satellite images and other tools to help study Earth.

## LEARNING FROM DISASTERS

In spite of careful planning, environmental disasters will occur. We must continue to learn from those disasters. Disasters have taught us important lessons. We can use those lessons in the years to come.

The disasters at Love Canal and Times Beach, for example, taught us that toxic waste was a problem. Our toxic waste storage systems weren't safe. It was too easy for toxic materials to escape.

People realized that we needed a law to clean up toxic waste dumps. The U.S. government made such a law. Called the Superfund, it provided money to help make toxic waste storage sites safer.

## SAFER TECHNOLOGY

Past disasters also have taught us how to avoid the accidents that often cause environmental disasters. After the *Exxon Valdez* disaster, the U.S. government made a new law about oil tankers. It said oil tankers must have a spill-resistant double hull by 2010.

The *Exxon Valdez* had one hull. When the hull was damaged, oil poured out of the ship. A ship with two hulls would not leak if only its outer hull were damaged. Its inner hull would hold toxic materials in and keep them from leaking.

The accident at the Three Mile Island nuclear power station in 1979 also led to improvements in safety. Three Mile Island led to safer nuclear power plants and better-trained workers.

**A worker suits up to begin his shift at the Three Mile Island nuclear power station in Pennsylvania. Safety has improved at power plants since the 1979 incident.**

NO
TRESPASSING

DANGEROUS
AREA

CITY OF NIAGARA FALLS. N. Y.

A fence and sign warn people away from the Love Canal toxic waste dump site in August 1978.

## WASTE SLURPERS

In the future, we may have better ways of reducing the damage in environmental disasters. New technology may make it easier to clean up oil spills and chemical leaks. For instance, scientists are trying to make helpful bacteria (germs) that could slurp up oil and toxic chemicals.

You may not think that bacteria could be helpful. But not all bacteria are the kind that make you sick. Some bacteria are good. Certain types of good bacteria use oil and toxic chemicals as food. They take nutrients from these hazardous substances.

Bacteria that eat hazardous substances can be used in bioremediation. Bioremediation is the treatment of pollution through the use of living organisms.

## SUPERSLURPERS

Bioremediation is not a new idea. But in the past, most chemical-eating bacteria had poor appetites. They ate too little or too slowly. It took them a long time to clean up dangerous materials.

New chemical eaters could be superslurpers. Scientists are trying to create superslurpers using genetic engineering. Genetic engineering is a way of choosing which traits a living thing inherits from its parents. Scientists want to change bioremediators into faster, bigger eaters. That way, they can use these special bacteria to clean up more disaster sites.

## AWARENESS—NOT WORRY

Environmental disasters have caused great damage. People have been injured and killed. Wild animals have been harmed. However, you should not let worry about an environmental disaster spoil your enjoyment of life. Environmental disasters are rare. And we're learning how to prevent these disasters and reduce the damage when a disaster happens.

Knowing about environmental disasters is important. It can help you prepare for a disaster and know what to do if a disaster happens. With that information, you can reduce the chance that you or a family member will be hurt in an environmental disaster.

# DISASTER SAFETY TIPS

Environmental disasters can strike without warning. To protect yourself, you must prepare. Here are some ways to stay safe in a chemical or nuclear emergency:

- Tune in to the local emergency response network or news station for information and instructions during any emergency.

- If told to evacuate, leave immediately. Follow directions from emergency officials, and do not panic.

- If told to "shelter in place," stay where you are. Leaving the building could be dangerous. Bring family members and pets inside. Close and lock all doors and windows. Turn off air conditioners and fans so that air from outside does not blow into your home. Close fireplace dampers. Stay in the basement or a room in the middle of the building. Tune to the local news or the emergency broadcast station for more instructions.

- If you may have been contaminated with a chemical or radioactive material, try to get emergency medical help. Dial 911 on the telephone. Some of the signs of chemical poisoning are trouble breathing; vomiting or diarrhea; dizziness; headache; blurred vision; and irritated eyes, skin, or throat.

- If no help is available, try to rinse the material off your skin and out of your eyes. Take off your clothing. Leave the clothing outside, or seal it in plastic so it cannot contaminate other people. Take a shower, and dress in clean clothing.

- If you see a disaster happening, call 911 immediately. Describe what happened and the number of people who are involved. Stay on the phone until the operator tells you to hang up.

# Timeline

**1272** King Edward I makes the first air pollution control law to reduce smog in London.

**1813** John James Audubon reports sighting huge flocks of passenger pigeons.

**1914** Martha, the world's last passenger pigeon, dies in the Cincinnati Zoo in Ohio on September 1.

**1932** A factory starts polluting the water of Minamata Bay in Japan with mercury. This poisonous material gets into fish in the bay. Thousands of people in Minamata still suffer from mercury poisoning in the twenty-first century.

**1952** Smoke from coal burning in stoves causes deadly smog to build up in London.

**1967** The *Torrey Canyon* oil spill near Great Britain causes about 30 million gallons (113 million l) of oil to pour into the ocean.

**1978** The *Amoco Cadiz* oil spill off the coast of Brittany, France *(right)*, pollutes 186 miles (299 km) of coastline.

A federal emergency is declared at the Love Canal site in Niagara Falls, New York.

**1979** Pumps break down at the Three Mile Island nuclear power plant near Harrisburg, Pennsylvania.

**1984** Toxic gas seeps from a chemical plant in Bhopal, India, killing and injuring thousands *(left)*. The effects of this chemical spill are still killing people in the Bhopal area.

**1986** Radioactive material leaks from the Chernobyl Nuclear Power Plant, devastating the land around the plant, as well as the lives of those who live there.

**1989** The *Exxon Valdez* oil spill kills and injures thousands of wild animals.

**2000** A gold mine in Baia Mare, Romania, accidentally spills the chemical cyanide into the Tisza River *(left)*, severely polluting the water supply.

The recession of the Aral Sea near Uzbekistan turns the city of Muynak into a desert.

**2002** The *Prestige*, a ship carrying oil, sinks off the coast of Spain, and black oil spills into the water. The water washes up on more than one thousand beaches across Spain and France.

**2004** Oil leaks from the *Selendang Ayu*, a ship sailing off the coast of Alaska. About 1,600 birds perish because of the leak.

**2005** Part of a chemical factory in the city of Jilin in northeastern China explodes *(right)*, and poison spills into the nearby water supply.

More than sixty countries start a project called GEOSS (Global Earth Observation System of Systems). The project allows scientists to observe Earth and potentially prevent future environmental disasters.

Hurricane Katrina causes more than 7 million gallons (27 million liters) of oil to spill in New Orleans.

**2006** Officials build a dam and canals to try to bring more water to the Aral Sea.

At least 20,000 tons (18,000 metric tons) of oil spill into the eastern Mediterranean Sea from a refinery in Jiyeh, Lebanon *(left)*.

**2007** A chemical spill cuts off water supplies to 200,000 residents of Shuyang County in eastern China.

# Glossary

**absorbent:** able to soak up liquids. Workers sometimes use absorbent materials to soak up oil after an oil spill.

**bioremediation:** the treatment of pollution through the use of living organisms

**boom:** a floating barrier that can keep spilled oil from spreading

**carbon dioxide:** a colorless, odorless gas that goes into the air when fossil fuels burn

**climate:** the usual kind or pattern of weather in a place over a long period of time

**crude oil:** oil in its natural state, before it has been processed so that people can use it

**dispersant:** a chemical that breaks oil into small droplets that quickly disappear

**evacuate:** to move to a safer place

**extinct:** having died out forever. If a species is extinct, it is no longer living on Earth.

**global warming:** the idea that Earth's climate is slowly getting warmer

**hazmat team:** a group of workers who are specially trained to respond to spills involving hazardous materials

**nuclear power plant:** a factory that uses radioactive material to make electricity

**ozone layer:** an invisible protective shield high in Earth's atmosphere. The ozone layer keeps harmful ultraviolet rays from reaching Earth's surface.

**pollution:** something that makes the land, air, or water dirty

**radioactive:** giving off particles of energy. Radioactive particles can be dangerous if they escape from a factory or plant.

**smog:** a kind of air pollution. *Smog* is a combination of the words *smoke* and *fog*.

**toxic:** poisonous

# Places to Visit

Black Creek Village—Niagara Falls, New York
http://www.epa.gov/history/topics/lovecanal/01.htm
Black Creek Village is the name for the area formerly known as Love Canal. Visitors to Black Creek Village can see the site from which two hundred and twenty one families were evacuated.

Cincinnati Zoo and Botanic Garden—Cincinnati, Ohio
http://www.goodzoos.com/USA/chicago1.htm
The Cincinnati Zoo features a memorial to Martha, the world's last passenger pigeon.

Prince William Sound Science Center—Cordova, Alaska
http://www.pwssc.gen.ak.us
Learn about the science center's Oil Spill Recovery Institute, which Congress created in response to the *Exxon Valdez* tragedy.

Route 66 State Park—Eureka, Missouri
http://www.legendsofamerica.com/MO-TimesBeach.html
Route 66 State Park was once the town of Times Beach, before a waste contractor sprayed toxic waste on the roads. The area has been decontaminated and is the site of Missouri's newest state park.

# Source Notes

4 Paul Welsh, "The Aral Sea Tragedy," *BBC News*, March 16, 2000, http://news.bbc.co.uk/1/hi/world/asia-pacific/678898.stm (May 19, 2006).

4–5 Khubbiniyaz Ashirbekov, quoted in Galima Bukharbaeva, "Aral Tragedy," *Institute for War & Peace Reporting*, June 9, 2000, http://www.iwpr.net/?p=rca&s=f&o=176211&apc_state=hruirca2000 (May 19, 2006).

5 Gaibull Mirzambekov, quoted in Galima Bukharbaeva, "Aral Tragedy," *Institute for War & Peace Reporting*, June 9, 2000, http://www.iwpr.net/?p=rca&s=f&o=176211&apc_state=hruirca2000 (May 19, 2006).

5 Paul Welsh, "The Aral Sea Tragedy," *BBC News*, March 16, 2000, http://news.bbc.co.uk/1/hi/world/asia-pacific/678898.stm (May 19, 2006).

7 Jose Carrapero, quoted in Adrian Croft, "Crews Battle to Stave Off Spain Oil Slick Disaster," *PlanetArk*, November 19, 2002, http://www.planetark.org/avantgo/dailynewsstory.cfm?newsid=18652 (June 21, 2007).

10 John James Audubon, quoted in Don Weiss, "In Memoriam: The Passenger Pigeon," *Ecotopia.org*, November 26, 2002, http://www.ecotopia.org/about/pigeon.html (June 19, 2006).

11 Ibid.

11 Mary Ellen Walker, quoted in Campbell Loughmiller and Lynn Loughmiller, *Big Thicket Legacy*, n.d., excerpted online at http://www.ulala.org/P_Pigeon/Texas.html (June 19, 2006).

19 Ahmed Khan, quoted in "On This Day: 3 December 1984: Hundreds Die in Bhopal Chemical Accident," *BBC News*, n.d., http://news.bbc.co.uk/onthisday/hi/dates/stories/december/3/newsid_2698000/2698709.stm (May 22, 2006).

22 Barbara Fewster, quoted in "Days of Toxic Darkness," *BBC News*, December 5, 2002, http://news.bbc.co.uk/1/hi/uk/2542315.stm (May 19, 2006).

23 Stan Cribb, quoted in John Nielsen, "The Killer Fog of '52," *NPR*, December 11, 2002, http://www.npr.org/templates/story/story.php?storyId=873954 (May 19, 2006).

23 Barry Linton, quoted in "Days of Toxic Darkness," *BBC News*, December 5, 2002, http://news.bbc.co.uk/1/hi/uk/2542315.stm (May 19, 2006).

23 Barbara Fewster, quoted in "Days of Toxic Darkness," *BBC News*, December 5, 2002, http://news.bbc.co.uk/1/hi/uk/2542315.stm (May 19, 2006).

23 Robert Waller, quoted in "Historic Smog Death Toll Rises," *BBC News*, December 5, 2002, http://news.bbc.co.uk/1/hi/health/2545747.stm (May 19, 2006).

23 Barbara Fewster, quoted in "Days of Toxic Darkness," *BBC News*, December 5, 2002, http://news.bbc.co.uk/1/hi/uk/2542315.stm (June 21, 2007).

28 Rashida Bee, quoted in Mark Hertsgaard, "Silent Night, Deadly Night," *AlterNet*, December 1, 2004, http://www.alternet.org/environment/20627 (June 21, 2007).

28 Champa Devi Shukla, quoted in Mark Hertsgaard, "Silent Night, Deadly Night," *AlterNet*, December 1, 2004, http://www.alternet.org/environment/20627 (June 21, 2007).

29 Champa Devi Shukla, quoted in "What Happened in Bhopal?," *The Bhopal Medical Appeal & Sambhavna Trust*, n.d., http://www.bhopal.org/whathappened.html (June 21, 2007).

29 Rashida Bee, quoted in Mark Hertsgaard, "Silent Night, Deadly Night," *AlterNet*, December 1, 2004, http://www.alternet.org/environment/20627 (June 21, 2007).

29 Aziza Sultan, quoted in "What Happened in Bhopal?" *The Bhopal Medical Appeal & Sambhavna Trust*, n.d., http://www.bhopal.org/whathappened.html (June 22, 2007).

33 Anatoly Zakharov, quoted in Dana Lewis, "Chernobyl: A Living Disaster," *Fox News*, April 25, 2006, http://www.foxnews.com/story/0,2933,192952,00.html (June 25, 2007).

36 Nadezhda Vygovskaya, quoted in Svetlana Alexievich, *Voices from Chernobyl: The Oral History of a Nuclear Disaster*, April 21, 2006, excerpted online at http://www.npr.org/templates/story/story/.php?storyId=5355810 (May 21, 2006).

37 Zhores Medvedev, *The Legacy of Chernobyl* (New York: W. W. Norton & Company, 1990), 142–143.

37 Zhores Medvedev, *The Legacy of Chernobyl* (New York: W. W. Norton & Company, 1990), 116.

45 Rick Steiner, quoted in Larry Campbell and Charles Wohlforth, "Rescuers, Cleanup Crews Tackle Vast Size of Spill," *Anchorage Daily News*, March 24, 1989.

46 Chuck O'Donnell, quoted in William C. Rempel, "Warnings Unheeded: Disaster at Valdez: Promises Unkept," *Los Angeles Times*, April 2, 1989.

47 Joseph Hazelwood, quoted in "*Exxon Valdez*: Hard Aground," *Living on Earth*, March 5, 1999, http://www.loe.org/series/exxon/aground.htm (June 26, 2007).

47 Dan Lawn, quoted in "*Exxon Valdez*: Hard Aground," *Living on Earth*, March 5, 1999, http://www.loe.org/series/exxon/aground.htm (May 19, 2006).

47 Jay Holcomb and Art Davidson, *In the Wake of the Exxon Valdez* (San Francisco: Sierra Club Books, 1990), 137.

47 Ibid.

# Selected Bibliography

Alexievich, Svetlana. *Voices from Chernobyl: The Oral History of a Nuclear Disaster*. New York: Picador, 2006.

Burger, Joanna. *Oil Spills*. New Brunswick, NJ: Rutgers University Press, 1997.

Davis, Lee. *Environmental Disasters: A Chronicle of Individual, Industrial, and Governmental Carelessness*. New York: Facts on File, 1998.

_____. *Man-Made Catastrophes*. New York: Facts on File, 2002.

Gunn, Angus M. *Unnatural Disasters: Case Studies of Human-Induced Environmental Catastrophes*. New York: Greenwood Press, 2003.

Keeble, John. *Out of the Channel: The* Exxon Valdez *Oil Spill in Prince William Sound*. Spokane, WA: Eastern Washington University Press, 1999.

Lapierre, Dominique, and Javier Moro. *Five Past Midnight in Bhopal*. New York: Warner Books, 2002.

Spignesi, Stephen J. *The 100 Greatest Disasters of All Time*. New York: Kensington Publishing Corp., 2002.

# Further Resources

## BOOKS

Bryan, Nichol. *Bhopal: Chemical Plant Accident*. Milwaukee: Gareth Stevens, 2004. Bryan writes a frightening account of the poison gas leak in Bhopal.

Fridell, Ron. *Global Warming*. New York: Franklin Watts, 2002. This clear and informative title examines the issue of global warming—a potential crisis for our environment.

Ingram, W. Scott. *The Chernobyl Nuclear Disaster*. New York: Facts on File, 2005. Ingram explains how the Chernobyl disaster occurred, how the government suppressed the information, and the tragic aftermath.

Lasky, Kathryn. *She's Wearing a Dead Bird on Her Head!* New York: Hyperion Books for Children, 1995. In the early twentieth century, the fashion was to wear dead birds atop fancy hats—but two Boston women were angered by the fad. This fun book contains a serious message about saving wild birds. It also discusses the history of the Massachusetts Audubon Society.

Leacock, Elspeth. *The* Exxon Valdez *Oil Spill*. New York: Facts on File, 2005. About 11 million gallons (42 million liters) of oil spilled in Prince William Sound, Alaska, when the *Exxon Valdez* accident occurred. Read all about it in this interesting selection.

Saunders, Nigel, and Steven Chapman. *Nuclear Energy*. Chicago: Raintree, 2005. Learn more about nuclear energy and how people use it.

Schlissel, Lillian. *Women's Diaries of the Westward Journey*. New York: Schocken Books, 1982. This is a collection of first-person accounts of families' journeys west in the nineteenth century. It includes descriptions of the prairie and native animals that became extinct.

Sepúlveda, Luis. *The Story of a Seagull and the Cat Who Taught Her to Fly*. New York: Arthur A. Levine Books, 2003. An oil-covered seagull asks Zorba the cat to grant her dying wish—to raise her chick.

Sherrow, Victoria. *The* Exxon Valdez: *Tragic Oil Spill*. Springfield, NJ: Enslow, 1998. This title on the *Exxon Valdez* oil spill includes an in-depth description of the event, firsthand accounts of the tragedy, and a chart comparing other oil tanker accidents.

Stanley, Jerry. *Children of the Dust Bowl: The True Story of the School at Weedpatch Camp*. New York: Crown, 1992. This book tells the story of those forced to move to California during the dust bowl disaster of the 1930s. In particular, it focuses on the residents of Weedpatch Camp, a farm labor camp built by the U.S. government.

# WEBSITES AND FILMS

**EPA Student Center**
http://www.epa.gov/students
The U.S. Environmental Protection Agency maintains this site to help students learn about their environment.

**The Feather Trade and the American Conservation Movement**
http://americanhistory.si.edu/feather/index.htm
The Smithsonian Institution has an online exhibit and explanation of the nineteenth-century fashion of using birds and animal skins as decorations.

**International Bird Rescue Research Center: How Oil Affects Birds**
http://www.ibrrc.org/oil_affects.html
This site is sponsored by the International Bird Rescue Research Center. It shows the effects of oil spills on birds.

**Prince William Sound: Paradise Lost?**
http://library.thinkquest.org/10867/home.shtml
Find out all about the *Exxon Valdez* oil spill.

**Species at Risk: Bison**
http://www.sierraclub.org/lewisandclark/species/bison.asp
The Sierra Club maintains this site with information about the history and the future of bison in the United States.

**Stacey Visits an Offshore Oil Rig**
http://www.mms.gov/mmskids/explore/explore.htm
On this site from the U.S. Department of the Interior Minerals Management Service, Stacey visits the oil rig where her dad works to find out what his job is all about.

**Three Mile Island**
http://hyperphysics.phy-astr.gsu.edu/hbase/nucene/tmi.html
Watch this slide show to see the events of the accident at Three Mile Island.

*Legacy of an Oil Spill*. DVD. Evanston, IL: Discovery Education, 2000. In this DVD, scientists explore the long-term effects of the *Exxon Valdez* oil spill.

*Turmoil in 20th Century Europe*. DVD. Evanston, IL: Discovery Education, 2004. This DVD explores twentieth-century disasters and events that changed Europe. It includes a brief segment on the nuclear accident at Chernobyl.

# Index

# Photo Acknowledgments

# About the Authors

Michael Woods is a science and medical journalist in Washington, D.C. He has won many national writing awards. Mary B. Woods is a school librarian. Their past books include the eight-volume Ancient Technology series. The Woodses have four children. When not writing, reading, or enjoying their grandchildren, they travel to gather material for future books.